# Celtic Treasure

'This beautiful book touches the heart-strings and gives us treasures of wisdom for our journey.'

'As you take in the beautiful illustrations and chosen text you will be transported into another world and enriched by our Celtic Christian heritage.'

*Dedicated to all my readers*
*in celebration of my tenth year as an author.*

# Celtic Treasure

## Unearthing the Riches of Celtic Spirituality

## Liz Babbs

Published in association with Alive
Communications Inc., 7680 Goddard Street,
Suite 200, Colorado Springs, CO 80920 USA,
www.alivecommunications.com

The author asserts the moral right
to be identified as the author of this work

A Lion Book
an imprint of
**Lion Hudson plc**
Wilkinson House, Jordan Hill Road,
Oxford OX2 8DR, England
www.lionhudson.com

ISBN 978 0 7459 5355 7 (UK)
ISBN 978 0 8254 7908 3 (US)

Distributed by:
UK: Marston Book Services, PO Box 269,
Abingdon, Oxon, OX14 4YN
USA: Trafalgar Square Publishing,
814 N. Franklin Street, Chicago, IL 60610
USA Christian Market: Kregel Publications,
PO Box 2607, Grand Rapids, Michigan
49501

First edition 2009

10 9 8 7 6 5 4 3 2 1 0

Typeset in Caxton BT
Printed and bound in China

**Picture Acknowledgments** p6 Michael
Sayles/Alamy; pp. 9, 12, 15, 17, 20, 27, 32,
34, 36, 39, 41, 42, 44, 46, 48, 57, 61, 65,
68, 71, 73, 74 iStock; p.18 Martin Gray/
Getty; p22 Digital Vision; p.33 Dynamic
Graphics; p.50 Bridgeman Art Library/Getty;
p.52 Stapleton Collection/Corbis; p.78 The
Irish Image Collection/Corbis

**Text Acknowledgments**
Every effort has been made to trace and acknowledge copyright
holders of all the quotations included. We apologize for any errors
or omissions that may remain, and would ask those concerned to
contact the publishers, who will ensure that full acknowledgment
is made in the future.
Scripture quotations marked NIV, and on back cover, are from
the *Holy Bible, New International Version*, copyright © 1973,
1978, 1984 International Bible Society. Used by permission of
Zondervan and Hodder & Stoughton Limited. All rights reserved.
The 'NIV' and 'New International Version' trademarks are
registered in the United States Patent and Trademark Office by
International Bible Society. Use of either trademark requires the
permission of International Bible Society. UK trademark number
1448790.
Scripture quotations marked GNB are from the *Good News Bible*
published by The Bible Societies/HarperCollins Publishers,
copyright © 1966, 1971, 1976, 1992 American Bible Society.
Scripture quotations marked CEV are from the Contemporary
English Version published by The Bible Societies/HarperCollins
Publishers, copyright © 1991, 1992, 1995 American Bible Society.
Scripture quotations marked NLT are taken from the *Holy Bible,
New Living Translation*, copyright © 1996. Used by permission
of Tyndale House Publishers, Inc., Wheaton, Illinois 60189. All
rights reserved.
Scripture quotations marked TM are from *The Message*. Copyright
© 1993, 1994, 1995, 1996, 2000, 2001, 2002. Used by
permission of NavPress Publishing Group.
Scripture quotations marked 'NKJV' are taken from the *New King
James Version*®. Copyright © 1982 by Thomas Nelson, Inc. Used
by permission. All rights reserved.
pp.24–25 and p.30 'The Prayer of St Aidan' are both from the
Brendan Liturgy and p.17 'St Aidan's Prayer for Lindisfarne',
all taken from *Celtic Daily Prayer*, Northumbria Community,
published by HarperCollins, 2000. p.32 'Smorring the Fire', p.34
'God to enfold me', p.55 'Caedmon' taken from *Carmina Gaedelica*
collected by Alexander Carmichael, published by Floris Books,
Edinburgh. p.33: 'Kindling the Fire' taken from *Celtic Fire*, Robert
Van de Weyer, Darton, Longman and Todd, London. p.36 'Circle
Me, Lord' by David Adam, from *The Edge of Glory*, published by
SPCK, London. p.56: 'Lover of My Soul', Cindy L Spear © 1997.
Used by permission.

The text paper used in this book has been made from wood
independently certified as having come from sustainable forests.
A catalogue record for this book is available
from the British Library.

9.16
3A

# CONTENTS

# INTRODUCTION

I keep a box of 'treasures' in my attic. These are personal possessions that are of little monetary value, but which remind me of a precious family member who has died. They are priceless 'treasures' that link me to the past, but also point me towards the future – my life is entwined with the lives of my family throughout generations. In a similar way, Christianity has an incredible spiritual heritage that stretches back not only through the generations but also across centuries. In the Bible, the life and death of Jesus in the New Testament only reveals its full significance when viewed through the lens of the Old Testament. The new always builds on the foundations of the old.

Many pilgrims exploring the ancient paths have gained insight and wisdom from the Celtic Christian tradition. I became interested in Celtic spirituality some years ago, drawn by its deep Christian heritage and the rich foundations laid by the saints. But it was when I attended a series of talks given by Roy Searle, one of the founding

**Your heart will always be where your treasure is.**
MATTHEW 6:21 [CEV]

leaders of The Northumbria Community – a network of people brought together by a sense of calling to the Celtic monastic legacy – that I was inspired to write *Celtic Treasure*, a gift book that uncovers some of the great riches of the Celtic way. In the busyness and confusion of our twenty-first century world, Celtic Christianity, with its holistic approach to finding God in all of life and its inclusive attitude to both men and women, offers a spirituality for our time. As the prophet Jeremiah reminds us:

**Stand at the crossroads and look;**
**ask for the ancient paths,**
**ask where the good way is, and walk in it,**
**and you will find rest for your souls.**
**JEREMIAH 6:16 [NIV]**

# UNEARTHING CELTIC TREASURE

**The life of a person leaves an imprint on the ether of a place.**

JOHN O'DONOHUE

Some years ago I spent an extended period of time travelling across Britain, visiting Scotland, Northumbria and Ireland while writing my first Celtic gift book, *The Celtic Heart*. As I journeyed from place to place I found myself increasingly drawn to, and inspired by, the radical faith and lifestyle of the Celtic saints. They have left a lasting impression on

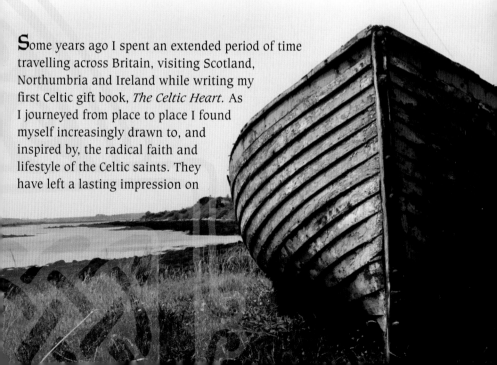

> Landscape has a secret and silent memory, a narrative of presence where nothing is ever lost or forgotten.
>
> JOHN O'DONOHUE

the landscape, and have touched the hearts of countless people across the centuries. When I sailed to Iona, in Scotland, I felt a profound sense of connection with these saints and the passion that fuelled their own spiritual journeys – even the difficulty we had anchoring that day reminded me of the dangers the saints had faced as they embarked upon the seas.

My next visit was to the stunningly beautiful tidal island of Lindisfarne. As I spent time there, I realized that though I had begun my trip as a tourist, I had become a pilgrim in search of 'the ancient paths'. My outward journey had led to a transformational inner journey that was changing the course of my writing.

Life is aptly described as a journey, but journeys involve risk as well as growth and change. The monks who once dwelt in the places I visited, some of whom have come to be remembered as the Celtic saints, risked their lives sailing on the open sea. Their coracles or curraghs were just small, light boats ribbed with wood and strengthened with iron and animal skins, but their passionate faith drove them to embark upon these voyages for the love of God. The dangers facing them were so great at times that they prayed special prayers for God's protection on the way. St Patrick's Breastplate Prayer is one of the most well known of these, and is still prayed and sung across Britain and Ireland today:

## ST PATRICK'S BREASTPLATE

I gird myself today and with the might of heaven:
The rays of the sun,
The beams of the moon,
The glory of fire,
The speed of wind,
The depth of sea,
The stability of earth,
The hardness of rock.

I gird myself today with the power of God:
God's strength to comfort me,
God's might to uphold me,
God's wisdom to guide me,
God's eye to look after me,
God's ear to hear me,
God's word to speak for me,
God's hand to lead me,
God's way to lie before me,
God's shield to protect me,
God's angels to save me.

From the snares of the Devil,
From temptations to sin,
From all who wish me ill,
Both far and near,
Alone and with others.

May Christ guard me today
From poison and fire,
From drowning and wounding,
So my mission may bear
Fruit in abundance.
Christ behind and before me,
Christ beneath and above me,
Christ with me and in me,
Christ around and about me,
Christ on my left and my right,
Christ when I rise in the morning,
Christ when I lie down at night,
Christ in each heart that thinks of me,
Christ in each eye that sees me,
Christ in each ear that hears me.

The Celtic saints, seeking to imitate Jesus, chose remote natural places where they could spend time alone with God in prayer. Celtic Christians believed that the veil between heaven and earth was 'thin' in these holy places and so it was easier to sense God's presence there. Pilgrims have continued to flock to these locations for centuries, not just because of their natural beauty, but also to walk the ancient pathways, in search of wisdom and enlightenment as they try to make sense of their lives. The Celtic 'thin' places of Iona and Lindisfarne have left a particular impression on myself and on many others.

> **Take off your sandals, for the place where you are standing is holy ground.**
> Exodus 3:5 [NIV]

**The purpose of pilgrimage is to tread in the shoes of Christ or his saints in order to make contact with the many rich experiences that are inevitable when we travel with him.**
Ray Simpson

**Blessed are those whose strength is in you, who have set their hearts on pilgrimage.**
Psalm 84:5 [NIV]

The island of Iona was home to St Columba and St Aidan. In AD 563, St Columba, along with twelve other men, founded a monastery that later became famous as a centre of mission. This Celtic monastic community remained on Iona until the thirteenth century, and was only dispersed when the Benedictine abbey was built there. The Benedictine settlement was subsequently destroyed during the Reformation, but amidst growing interest in Celtic Christianity in the twentieth century, the abbey was rebuilt. In 1938, Reverend George MacLeod visited and founded The Iona Community, a new monastic community that is still active today. Fiona MacLeod wrote of Iona in *The Divine Adventurer*:

A few places in the world are to be held holy… One such is Iona… It is but a small isle, fashioned of a little sand, a few grasses salt with the spray of an ever-restless wave, a few rocks that wade in heather, and upon whose brows the sea-wind weaves the yellow lichen. But since the remotest days, sacrosanct men have bowed here in worship. In this little island a lamp was lit whose flame lighted pagan Europe. From age to age, lowly hearts have never ceased to bring their burden here. And here Hope waits. To tell the story of Iona is to go back to God, and to end in God.

# IONA

A place to lose yourself
A place to find yourself
A place of journey's end
A place of journey's beginning.

LIZ BABBS

Lindisfarne is sometimes called 'the holiest place in England', and it has even become known as Holy Island, because so many saints have lived there. It has also been described as the 'cradle of British Christianity' and is a place of immense historic and religious significance. Describing this tidal island, St Bede wrote:

**As the tide ebbs and flows, this place is surrounded twice daily by the waves of the sea like an island, and twice, when the sands are dry, it becomes again attached to the mainland.**

Lindisfarne's rich Christian heritage dates back to AD 635 with the foundation of the first monastery. It was from this monastery that early missionaries, led by St Aidan and St Cuthbert, spread the Christian faith throughout the whole of northern Britain, and in time it became famous also as a centre for learning and for the training of missionary priests, until Viking attacks forced the monks to leave in the ninth century. Monks from Durham Cathedral returned in the twelfth century and founded a Benedictine priory that flourished there until 1537, when Henry VIII closed it. However, several communities representing a new form of monasticism continue in this rich tradition today, including The Community of Aidan and Hilda and The Northumbria Community. They walk in the footsteps of Aidan, continuing on a path that has been walked for 1,300 years, and this prayer, written in the spirit of Aidan, continues to be prayed daily on the island:

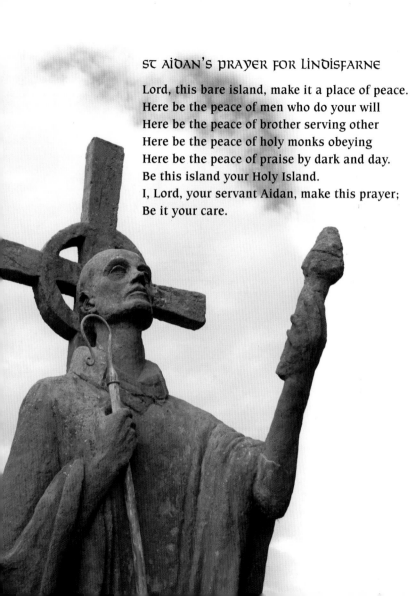

## ST AIDAN'S PRAYER FOR LINDISFARNE

Lord, this bare island, make it a place of peace.
Here be the peace of men who do your will
Here be the peace of brother serving other
Here be the peace of holy monks obeying
Here be the peace of praise by dark and day.
Be this island your Holy Island.
I, Lord, your servant Aidan, make this prayer;
Be it your care.

Visiting Lindisfarne is a joy, because as soon as you set foot on the island, you know you are standing on holy ground. Sensing the timeless presence of God, prayer seems to flow as naturally as breathing. Lindisfarne is also a place that stimulates creativity. From the depths of this connection, poetry and prayers flow.

## ON LINDISFARNE

On Lindisfarne
walking in the ancient footsteps
of Saint Cuthbert
I know I am standing
on Holy Ground.
Sacred steps that prayed,
surrendered,
sacrificed,
saved.
And their memory lingers on...
An inspirational presence
saturating the landscape
with the holiness
of the one
true
God.

LIZ BABBS

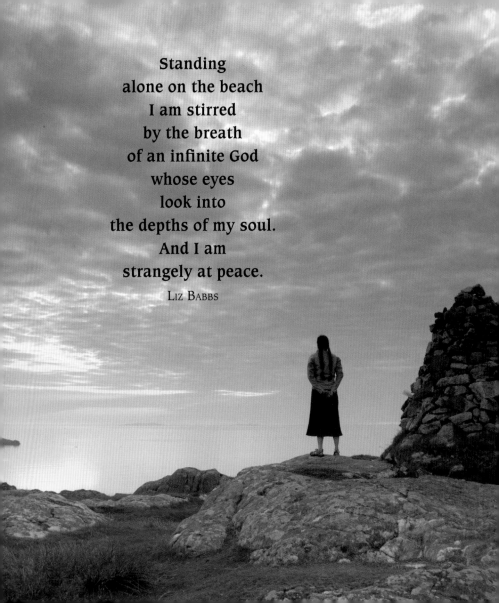

Standing
alone on the beach
I am stirred
by the breath
of an infinite God
whose eyes
look into
the depths of my soul.
And I am
strangely at peace.

LIZ BABBS

# CELTIC SAINTS

**A saint is one who exaggerates
what the world neglects.**

G. K. CHESTERTON

The Celtic saints brought Christianity to
Britain and extended their reach into Europe in
the fourth century. The Roman retreat allowed Celtic
spirituality in Britain the freedom to develop outside
Roman rule. The Celts had at times struggled with
tendencies on the part of the Roman Church to be
controlling of their beliefs and practices, as well as
being negative towards the involvement of women;
their withdrawal allowed Celtic Christianity to flourish
as a 'church without walls', where monks, travelling
by land and sea, set up communities wherever they
landed. These communities celebrated the loving
presence of God in the whole of life, as this prayer
attributed to St Patrick reveals:

> Go to the people of all nations and make them my disciples. Baptize them in the name of the Father, the Son and the Holy Spirit.
>
> **MATTHEW 28:19 [CEV]**

I arise today
Through the strength of heaven:
Light of Sun,
Radiance of moon,
Splendour of fire,
Speed of lightening,
Swiftness of wind,
Depth of sea,
Stability of earth,
Firmness of rock.

The Celtic monastic life drew deeply upon the tradition of the desert fathers and mothers, a group of fourth-century Christians living in Egypt who felt called to leave the corruption of the city to live solitary lives of prayer, meditation and fasting in the desert. It was from this background that Celtic monasteries emerged, the vehicle both of Celtic Christianity and of a transformation of the culture from the edges of society. Owing to these communities' passion for equality and justice, women were granted rights they would not have enjoyed in other societies, many finding themselves in positions of leadership.

The Celtic monks and nuns lived harsh lives characterized by abstinence from worldly pleasure. They were prepared to give up everything including money, homes and families to go wherever God called them. They devoted themselves to God and prayed without ceasing, relying on his protection and provision. Travelling by sea far from home, they trusted that wherever they landed, God had sent them.

The Celtic Christians spoke of different levels of martyrdom. The life of sacrificial pilgrimage they termed 'green' martyrdom, but many monks also suffered the 'red' martyrdom of death for their beliefs. **St Brendan** (c. AD 484–577) was an Irish monk who moved from place to place founding monastic cells and communities. He is said to have travelled the farthest of all the saints, and some say he even sailed across the Atlantic to Newfoundland. This radical lifestyle is recalled in a moving prayer from Northumbria Community's Brendan Liturgy:

Shall I abandon, O King of Mysteries, the soft comforts of home? Shall I turn my back on my native land and my face towards the sea?

Shall I put myself wholly at the mercy of God, without silver, without a horse, without fame and honour? Shall I throw myself wholly on the King of kings, without sword and shield, without food and drink, without a bed to lie on?

Shall I say farewell to my beautiful land, placing myself under Christ's yoke? Shall I pour out my heart to him, confessing my manifold sins and begging forgiveness, tears streaming down my cheeks?

Shall I leave the prints of my knees on the sandy beach, a record of my final prayer in my native land? Shall I then suffer every kind of wound that the sea can inflict?

Shall I take my tiny coracle across the wide, sparkling ocean? O King of the Glorious Heaven, shall I go of my own choice upon the sea?

O Christ, will you help me on the wild waves?

**St Ninian** (c. AD 360-432), was the first great saint of the Celtic Church. Ninian set up a monastery at Whithorn in Scotland which became the model for communities of monks and nuns across the Celtic lands.

The monastery was at the heart of Celtic spirituality. A hermit would build himself a hut and then others would join and build additional huts and a chapel. These communities would grow as people were attracted to them and could consist of hundreds or even thousands of people. Some of the monks were even married. These larger communities would give birth to new communities as monks and nuns travelled to set up new monasteries.

**St Patrick** (AD 387–461) is possibly the most famous Irishman of all time. However, he was not actually born in Ireland, but in a place called Bonna venta Berniae. The exact location is not known and varies from being a town in the north west of England to Kilpatrick in what is now Scotland. He was the son of a deacon and worked on his father's farm as a young boy. At the age of sixteen he was captured by raiders and sold into slavery in Ireland. Six years later, Patrick escaped, having been shown how by God in a vision. He returned to his family, and began to embrace a monastic way of life. In time he became a priest. Some years later God called him back to Ireland, where he eventually became bishop. Many stories have been told of Patrick's travels across Ireland, preaching and converting people as he went. Irish people all around the world celebrate his achievements on 17 March, which is said to be the anniversary of his death. This extract from St Patrick's *Declaration* gives a wonderful insight into his life:

After coming to Ireland I was put to work tending cattle, sheep and hogs, and many times during that day I would pray. More and more the love of God and the fear of God came to me, so that my faith was strengthened and my spirit moved. In a single day I would pray as often as a hundred times, and nearly as often at night, when I was staying in the woods and the mountains, I would rouse myself before daylight to pray, whether in snow, frost, or rain; it made no difference, and I felt no bad effects. Because the Spirit in me was fervent, I knew no sluggishness.

**St Brigid** (AD 450–523) is regarded as the female patron saint of Ireland. St Patrick baptized her parents and she developed a close relationship with him. Her passion in life was for the poor and when she was only nine she is said to have taken the jewels from her father's new sword and given them to hungry peasants. The king, who had given Brigid's father the sword as a special gift, was understandably angry, but Brigid responded with the reflection that to give to the poor is to give to Christ himself, who is of even higher authority than a king.

Brigid became a nun and in AD 470 founded a double monastery – for both men and women – at Kildare and became abbess of the first convent in Ireland. Brigid also became famous for her many miracles; the sick were said to have been healed by touching her cloak.

## Brigid's Blessing

Every day I pray to St Brigid that...

No fire, no flame shall burn me;
No lake, no sea shall drown me;
No sword, no spear shall wound me;
No king, no chief insult me.

All birds shall sing for me;
All the cattle low for me;
All the insects buzz for me;
God's angels shall protect me.

**St Columba** (AD 521–597) was born in Ireland and when he was a child he gave away all his wealth to become a monk. Although his name means dove, he is said to have struggled with his temper and as a result of a major disagreement with the Irish Church, sailed to Iona. He set up a monastery there which became a missionary base from which Christianity spread throughout Scotland and northern England. This prayer attributed to Columba offers a wonderful insight into the depth of his faith in God.

Let me bless the almighty God,
whose power extends over sea and land
and whose angels watch over all.
Let me study sacred books to calm my soul.
I pray for peace, kneeling at heaven's gates.
Let me do my daily work, gathering seaweed,
catching fish, giving food to the poor.
Let me say my daily prayers, sometimes chanting,
sometimes quiet, always thanking God.
Delightful it is to live on a peaceful isle, in a quiet cell,
serving the King of kings.

**St Aidan** (died AD 651) was born in Ireland, but became a monk at Iona. He was said to have been of a very gentle disposition and was described by St Bede as a man who 'cultivated peace and love, purity and humility'. He was sent by King Oswald to Northumbria to re-establish the Church in his kingdom and was made bishop in AD 635, choosing Lindisfarne as his base. It is said that King Oswin gave Aidan a horse to aid him in his missionary journeys, which Aidan subsequently gave to a beggar who was in need. In any case, a horse would have given Aidan a higher status than those who he was ministering to, contrary to his desire to be a man of the people, treating all equal and setting slaves free whenever he could. He also valued his solitude and successfully managed to combine the monastic lifestyle with missionary journeys to the mainland. This prayer in the spirit of St Aidan is a particular favourite with many:

## The Prayer of St Aidan

Leave me alone with God as much as may be.
As the tide draws the waters close in upon the shore,
Make me an island, set apart,
alone with you, God, holy to you.

Then with the turning of the tide
prepare me to carry your presence to the busy world beyond,
the world that rushes in on me
till the waters come again and fold me back to you.

**St Cuthbert** (c. AD 635–687) started life as a simple shepherd boy, but was called by God to be a major Christian leader. He is another of the great heroes of Celtic monasticism and was inspired by King David's life and writings in the Psalms. Said to have been born in Scotland he, like Aidan, was reputed to be a man of great faith and gentleness. He entered monastic life at Melrose Abbey, in Scotland, from where he began his missionary work. He walked the countryside talking about his faith to anyone he met and many healing miracles were associated with him. He became abbot of Lindisfarne, and later became a hermit on the island of Farne. In 685 he was elected bishop of Lindisfarne and continued to travel and preach all over his diocese, but after two years he became very ill and returned to his beloved Farne to die. Eleven years after his death St Cuthbert's coffin was exhumed and the monks found that miraculously his body had not decayed. Consequently, pilgrims flocked to his tomb believing they could be healed. These words from St Cuthbert form one of the best-known Celtic prayers.

My dearest Lord,
Be thou a bright flame before me,
Be thou a guiding star above me,
Be thou a smooth path beneath me,
Be thou a kindly shepherd behind me,
Today and for evermore.

# Chapter 3

# PRAYER AND SOLITUDE

The Celts believed that God was with them in every aspect of their daily lives. Whatever the task or time of day, there was a special prayer to be said, whether milking a cow or kindling a fire:

### SMOORING THE FIRE

The sacred Three
To save,
To surround
The hearth,
The household,
This eve,
This night,
Oh! this eve,
This night,
And every night,
Each single night.
Amen.

CARMINA GADELICA

# Kindling the Fire

This morning, as I kindle the fire upon the hearth,
I pray that the flame of God's love may burn in
my heart,
and the hearts of all I meet today.
I pray that no envy and malice, no hatred or fear,
may smother the flame.
I pray that indifference and apathy, contempt and pride,
may not pour like cold water on the fire.
Instead, may the spark of God's love
light the love in my heart,
that it may burn brightly through the day.
And may I warm those that are lonely,
whose hearts are cold and lifeless,
so that all may know the comfort of God's love.

Such prayers were exchanged in everyday life. A modern workplace equivalent might be to include a short prayer within the body of a letter or an email. Much of the prayer of the Celtic Church would have been spontaneous like this and simple to learn:

God to enfold me, God to surround me,
God in my speaking, God in my
thinking,
God in my sleeping, God in my waking,
God in my watching, God in my hoping,
God in my life, God in my lips,
God in my soul, God in my heart,
God in my sufficing, God in my slumber,
God in mine ever-living soul,
God in mine eternity.

CARMINA GADELICA

Trinitarian prayers were also popular and as a housewife cut the sign of the cross in the dough she would bless it. When milking the cow, the first drop of milk was used to bless the cow 'in the name of the Father and of the Son and the Holy Spirit'. The ending of St Patrick's Breastplate Prayer also emphasizes the Celts' strong relationship with the Trinity:

### ST PATRICK'S BREASTPLATE

I bind unto myself the Name,
the strong Name of the Trinity,
by invocation of the same,
the Three in One,
and One in Three,
of Whom all nature hath creation;
Eternal Father, Spirit, Word:
praise to the Lord of my salvation,
salvation is of Christ the Lord.
Amen.

'Caim' or 'encircling' prayers were recited too. The Celts used these prayers to affirm the presence of God and to remind them of his protection. While praying they would draw an invisible circle around themselves with their right index finger, extending their arm towards the ground while turning clockwise. Here are some examples of this type of prayer:

Circle me, Lord
Keep hope within
And despair without.

Circle me, Lord
Keep light near
And darkness afar.

Circle me, Lord
Keep peace within
And anxiety without.

DAVID ADAM

Encircling arms of the Creator Father – I belong to you,
All embracing love of Jesus the Son –
I belong to you,
Empowering presence of the Holy Spirit –
I belong to you.

LIZ BABBS

Celtic prayer also shows an awareness of the presence of angels and their involvement in both the supernatural and the natural realms of life. The poem 'Angel Voices' was inspired by the ancient tradition of choral evensong:

## ANGEL VOICES

Angel voices ring out around these
ancient cloistered passageways
embodying creation's praise.
And harmonised prayer
borne on Spirit wings
rises heavenwards
as incense to a
most Holy
God.

LIZ BABBS

The spirituality of the Celts was earthed both in solitude and in community. They did not see one aspect of their faith as separate from the other, but wove them together. Monks lived alone in 'cells', which were basic stone huts where they could pray. But solitude in the monastic tradition did not cut a person off from the real world, but rather brought them more in tune with it. A contemporary definition of the life of a monk offered by Ray Simpson, guardian of the Community of Aidan and Hilda, is 'one who separates from everybody in order to be reunited to everyone', as these words express:

**Whether the sun is at its height, or the moon and stars pierce the darkness, my little hut is always open. It shall never be closed to anyone, lest I should close it to Christ himself.**

St Cuthbert lived much of his life as a hermit and later moved to the island of Inner Farne. But however isolated he was, he still struggled with worldly temptations as he describes below:

**Even if I could possibly hide myself away in a tiny dwelling on a rock, where the waves of the swelling ocean surround me on all sides, and shut me in**

completely from the sight and knowledge of men, not even there should I consider myself free from the snares of this deceptive world; but I should fear least the love of wealth might tempt me and somehow still snatch me away.

The following prayer was inspired by visiting St Cuthbert's Island, the secluded tidal island alongside the Lindisfarne Priory, where Cuthbert used to retreat to pray:

> Lord, make me an island
> set apart for you.
> Where the rock of ages
> rings out with praise.
> Where the waters of your spirit
> saturate my soul
> And the fire of your presence
> burns deep within.

LIZ BABBS

Just as in our Western culture people currently seek out the wisdom of spiritual gurus, centuries ago many were searching for direction in their lives, and were drawn to the Celtic monks and nuns. That tradition continues today, as many Christians, have nuns or monks as spiritual directors or soul friends. The Celtic idea of an *anam cara*, Gaelic words meaning 'soul friend', embodies the notion of a deeply nurturing spiritual friendship. An *anam cara* was someone you could share your deepest thoughts with, your innermost self, and receive guidance and wisdom for the spiritual journey. John O'Donohue, a former Irish priest and philosopher, writes in his book *Anam Cara*:

> **When you are blessed with an anam cara…you have arrived at that most sacred place: home… You are joined in an ancient and eternal union with humanity that cuts across all barriers of time, convention, philosophy and definition.**

# 4

For since the creation of the world God's invisible qualities – his eternal power and divine nature – have been clearly seen, being understood from what has been made.

**ROMANS 1:20 [NIV]**

# GOD OF CREATION

More things are learned in the woods than from books. Animals, trees and rocks teach you things not to be heard elsewhere.

ST BERNARD

> The earth is the Lord's, and everything in it,
>    the world, and all who live in it;
>       for he founded it upon the seas
>          and established it upon the waters.
>
> PSALM 24:1–2 [NIV]

The Celtic Christians did not worship creation like
their pagan counterparts, but rather praised the God of
creation, who in the book of Genesis, breathed life into a
body formed from dust to create the first human being.
Although the Celts knew that the Bible was the ultimate
revelation of God, nature became a secondary revelation,
and many saw creation as a reflection of heaven. The
legends say that when a Celtic princess asked St Patrick
who God was and where his dwelling could be found,
Patrick replied:

> Our God, God of all men,
> God of heaven and earth, seas and rivers,
> God of sun and moon, of all the stars,
> God of high mountains and of lowly valleys,
> God over heaven, and in heaven, and under heaven.
> He has a dwelling in heaven and earth and sea
> and in all things that are in them.
> He inspires all things, He quickens all things,
> He is over all things, He supports all things...

For the Celts, study involved far more than just traditional learning – it encompassed the natural world too. St Ninian wrote that the fruit of study was 'to perceive the eternal Word of God reflected in every plant and insect, every bird and animal, and every man and woman'.

Many of the Celtic saints were hermits and they chose some of the most beautiful locations to live in solitude

and prayer. These places were often also sanctuaries for birds and wildlife. The saints lived their lives in harmony with the seasons. Touched by the beauty of the natural world, their prayers became poetry and praise, such as this one attributed to St Columba:

Lord, you are my island
In your bosom I nest.
You are the calm of the sea
In that peace I rest.
You are the waves on the shore's
glistening stones
Their sound is my hymn.
You are the song of the birds
Their tune I sing.
You are the sea breaking on rock
I Praise you with the swell.
You are the ocean that laps my being
In you I dwell.

Celtic Christians cared about the environment in which they lived and rejoiced in creation, appreciating the delicate balance between human beings and nature. They did not separate the creator from all he had created, but worshipped God through the natural world. Like the well-known Celtic symbol, the Celtic knot, they could see God woven into everything.

## CELTIC WEAVE
My whole being is earthed in You
Creator God.
For I am part of your infinite
circle of continuity.
You heal the rings of my
uncertainty
and weave love
into the fabric of my experience.
My whole being is earthed in You
Creator God,
my Father,
my Lord
my God.

LIZ BABBS

Spirit of God around me
In the air that I breathe.

Glory of God around me
Inspiring all I see.

Joy of God around me
In laughter and in mirth.

Majesty of God around me
In the fruitfulness of the earth.

Son of God around me
In the creatures of this land.

Love of God around me
Holding my future in his hands.

LIZ BABBS

The Celtic cross, which is a well-known symbol of
Celtic Christianity combining a circle and a cross,
wonderfully illustrates the way the earth and the cross
and resurrection have been integrated. Many Celtic
standing crosses also depict scenes from the Bible. This
visual portrayal of faith though art and symbol was very
important, since most Celts would not have been able
to read.

Celtic Christians drew much inspiration from the teachings of St John, viewing him in many ways as a spiritual father. John had a very close relationship with Jesus and was described as 'the disciple whom Jesus loved' (John 13:23). John's gospel emphasizes Christ as the one who created and sustains the universe, perhaps one of the reasons the Celts had such reverence for creation.

Before the world was created, the Word already existed... Through him God made all things... the Word became a human being.
JOHN 1:1, 3, 14 [GNB]

**Nature is a universal language through which God has spoken to his people across the generations. It is his great love letter to us.**

LIZ BABBS

It is not just the natural world that was relished, but its inhabitants too. The Celts believed that animals were a great blessing to them. Many Celtic saints had special relationships with the animals, so much so that it is thought that during these times animals were first brought into homes and domesticated. It is said that otters used to warm and dry the feet of St Cuthbert when he would wade out into the sea to pray during his all night vigils. Legend also has it that while St Kevin of Glendalough was praying one day a blackbird laid her eggs in the palm of his hand. He remained in that position until the eggs hatched; such was the reverence of the Celtic saints for the natural world. Even a horse is said to have laid its head on St Columba's chest and shed tears while he was dying. Celtic poems and prayers have also traditionally compared the Holy Spirit to a Wild Goose:

> Great Spirit, Wild Goose of the Almighty,
> Be my eye in the dark places;
> Be my flight in the trapped places;
> Be my host in the wild places;
> Be my brood in the barren places
> Be my formation in the lost places.
>
> RAY SIMPSON

> Stirred by the breath of the infinite God,
> the Holy Spirit
> whispers
> through desert sands
> hovers
> over shimmering waters,
> rises
> on heaven's wings.
>
> LIZ BABBS

Hear my cry, O God; listen to my prayer... For you have been my refuge, a strong tower against the foe. I long to dwell in your tent forever and take refuge in the shelter of your wings.

PSALM 61:1, 3, 4 [ESV]

49

# CELEBRATING CREATIVITY

For we are God's masterpiece. He has created us anew in Christ Jesus, so we can do the good things he planned for us long ago.
**EPHESIANS 2:10 [NLT]**

Centuries ago, the Celts entertained themselves with stories, songs, art, dance and poetry. They were highly creative people, producing pottery and woodwork, excelling at metalwork including weapons and elaborate jewellery. Celtic art was characterized by richly decorated flowing curves, often based on animal and plant motifs. In Britain and Ireland, Celtic art blossomed still further with the coming of Christianity, producing sculpture including elaborately carved crosses depicting stories from the Bible and creating exquisitely beautiful illuminated manuscripts.

The *Lindisfarne Gospels* is an illuminated manuscript of the four Gospels in Latin. The manuscript was meticulously copied by monks on Lindisfarne in the late seventh century, possibly in honour of St Cuthbert, and was encased in fine leather and jewels. The *Book of Kells* is another example and was worked on at St Columba's famous monastery on Iona, possibly also in honour of him. The name is derived from the abbey of

Kells, in Ireland, which was its home for many centuries. It contains the four Gospels in Latin and is highly ornate combining traditional Christian iconography with highly decorative swirls and motifs containing Christian symbolism. The *Lindisfarne Gospels*, together with the *Book of Kells*, are considered to be the finest examples of this Celtic style of religious art. Artist Mary Fleeson continues this rich tradition on Lindisfarne today, at the Lindisfarne Scriptorium, drawing on the spiritual and visual inspiration of the monks, but using modern materials and techniques. In so doing, she is following in the footsteps of the great monastic scriptorium tradition of producing artwork that gives glory to God.

The Celts loved storytelling; many of their stories were handed down in the form of songs and poems from one generation to another. In this way they imitated Jesus, the most famous storyteller that ever lived. He used stories to explain the message of God in a contemporary way and so earthed theology in people's daily lives. For the Celts, stories that could be passed on orally were essential, since most were unable to read. This meant that people could hear and experience the life and teachings of Jesus. Telling stories is a very communal activity and many, including members of The Northumbria Community, continue this rich tradition today.

Fathers were said to pass the gift of storytelling to their sons and poetry to their daughters, and storytellers and poets were held in high esteem. This poem attributed to St David, patron saint of Wales, highlights the Celts' love of poetry:

**No man is the son of knowledge if he is not also**
**the son of poetry.**
**No man loves poetry without loving the light,**
**Nor the light without loving the truth,**
**Nor the truth without loving justice,**
**Nor justice without loving God.**

The Psalms have been described as the songbook of the Bible. The Celts would have memorized these prayers and sung or recited them during the course of their day. The Psalms express in poetry every possible human emotion from despair to praise. Jesus, when he was dying on the cross, cried out from Psalm 22 'My God, my God, why have you abandoned me?' The Psalms have been central to Christian worship across the centuries and continue to be a great source of comfort to people today, inspiring countless songs.

Praise the Lord!

Praise God in his sanctuary;
praise him in his mighty heaven!
Praise him for his mighty works;
praise his unequalled greatness!
Praise him with a blast of the ram's horn;
praise him with the lyre and harp!
Praise him with the tambourine and dancing;
praise him with strings and flutes!
Praise him with a clash of cymbals;
Praise God with loud clanging cymbals.
Let everything that breathes sing praises to the Lord!

Praise the Lord!

PSALM 150:1–6 [NLT]

54

Celtic music evolved out of the folk music traditions of the peoples of northern Europe, with songs probably passed from one generation to another through the oral tradition, just as the stories and poems had been. St Bede told the story of a poet called Caedmon, who when the harp was being passed round after supper, left the room in embarrassment because he could not sing. When he fell asleep, an angel appeared to him in a dream asking him to sing a song. Caedmon refused, but the angel asked him again and this time he asked, 'But what will I sing?' The angel answered, 'Sing me the creation.' Later Caedmon composed and sang a hymn in his sleep. This was the first of many he would become famous for composing.

Grace of form,
Grace of voice be thine.
Grace of life,
Grace of praise be thine;
Grace of love,
Grace of dancing be thine;
Grace of lyre,
Grace of harp be thine;
Grace of sense,
Grace of reason be thine;
Grace of speech,
Grace of story be thine;
Grace of peace,
Grace of God be thine.

CARMINA GADELICA

Today many bands, with a variety of old and new musical styles, keep the Celtic music and Irish folk tradition alive across the world. One of the most successful Celtic Christian bands in Britain is Iona. The vision for this internationally renowned Celtic rock band was born out of a transformational visit to Iona and Lindisfarne. Visiting these holy Celtic islands continues to have a profound effect upon artists, stirring their creativity and enriching their faith. Canadian lyricist and poet Cindy L. Spear has written some beautiful lyrics for Iona, including 'Lover of My Soul':

### Lover of my soul

The gentle ebb and flow of ocean
Soothes my weary soul this eve.
I stand and watch the moonlight dancing
Silver crests on emerald sea.

Your breath is blowing soft upon me,
Like the wind upon the harp;
The cloak of night begins to tremble
The wild goose cries out from the dark.

As I kneel upon this altar
A wreath of stones, a sacred place
I feel the sweetness of your presence
And touch the glory of your face.

I open up my heart before you
A broken alabaster jar
To pour my fears and all my sorrows
Upon the shore, beneath the stars.

O Lover of my soul, my passion,
Come and fill me now, make haste;
I will trust the Lord of my salvation
My Hope and Joy, my Song and Strength.

When the Celts arrived in Britain from Ireland and central Europe, they brought with them their own folk dances. A ceilidh is a traditional Gaelic social dance originating in Ireland and Scotland, but which is now popular throughout the world. Originally, a ceilidh was a social gathering that could include stories, songs, poems, proverbs, ballads, and need not necessarily feature dance. As the Celts celebrated the whole of life, dance was a natural part of that celebration. In the Bible, King David danced in worship of God. Andy Raine, one of the Founders of The Northumbria Community, continues this tradition by leading men in dance and movement across the UK. Andy's dances interpret in movement and worship themes such as the prayer St Patrick's Breastplate, the encircling caim prayers and the lives of the saints. His approach is both prayerful and dynamic, and so it is not surprising that he has inspired many men to dance as David would have danced before the Lord.

## SACRED TAPESTRY

Each person
a precious thread
open ended with
creative possibility
and when linked to others
weaves a community
of beauty –
a sacred tapestry
mirroring heaven.

LIZ BABBS

**The dance of life
The circle of joy
The intimacy of the Creator
both Father and Lord.**

LIZ BABBS

# CHAPTER 6

# VALUING COMMUNITY

He alone loves the Creator perfectly who manifests
a pure love for his neighbour.

ST BEDE

Genesis tells us that there is only one thing that is not
good for humanity, and that is for a person to be alone.
Unfortunately, the Western world has become increasingly
individualistic and our work-obsessed, consumerist
culture leaves us with little time to make or maintain
friendships and relationships. Nevertheless, people still
search for community, whether in the real world or on the
Internet.

Similarly, our individualistic culture has replaced
seeking spiritual counsel with self-help books that
dominate the bestseller lists and which have become the
wisdom literature of our age. The Bible reminds us we
are 'one body, many parts'; in other words, we are created
to need each other. For those seeking the Celtic way of

> The body is a unit, though it is made up of many parts; and though all its parts are many, they form one body... If one part suffers, every part suffers with it; if one part is honoured, every part rejoices with it. Now you are the body of Christ, and each one of you is part of it.
>
> 1 CORINTHIANS 12:12, 26–27 [NIV]

wisdom, the treasures lie in ancient texts of the Bible and the inspirational writings of the saints.

Building community remains central to Celtic spirituality. The Celts understood that their relationship with God and each other was at the heart of the Gospel message. When Jesus was asked for the most important commandment, he said: '"You must love him with all your heart, soul, mind, and strength." The second most important commandment says: "Love others as much as you love yourself." No other commandment is more important than these' (Mark 12:30–31). Jesus also said that it was through the love his followers displayed for one another that people would know they were his disciples' (John 13:34–35). That is not to say, of course, that they never disagreed with each other, but rather that the way they conducted themselves, whether in agreement or disagreement, was characterized by love.

> For love is of God.
> It's the life force shaping all creation.
> The very essence we breathe.
> For love removes boundaries
> eradicates prejudice
> crosses divides
> builds community
> and moulds
> history.
>
> LIZ BABBS

Celtic Christians sought to live out, as a community, a spirituality founded upon the Beatitudes. These radical teachings of Jesus given in the Sermon on the Mount are sometimes referred to as the 'Beautiful Attitudes':

God blesses those people who depend only on him.
They belong to the kingdom of heaven!
God blesses those people who grieve.
They will find comfort!
God blesses those people who are humble.
The earth will belong to them!
God blesses those people who want to obey him more than to eat or drink.
They will be given what they want!
God blesses those people who are merciful.
They will be treated with mercy!
God blesses those people whose hearts are pure.
They will see him!
God blesses those people who make peace.
They will be called his children!
God blesses those people who are treated badly for doing right.
They belong to the kingdom of heaven.

MATTHEW 5:3–10 [NLT]

## CONTEMPORARY BEATITUDES

To those who are lost
And ache for truth,
God brings his comfort.

To those who cry out for justice
But have no proof,
God brings his comfort.

To those who struggle to
Make ends meet,
God brings his comfort.

To those who don't have
Enough to eat,
God brings his comfort.

To those who are marginalized
And have no self worth,
God brings his comfort.

Liz Babbs

The Celtic model for Christian community
was God as a welcoming, loving family of
three persons – Father, Son and Holy Spirit.

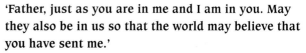

'Father, just as you are in me and I am in you. May
they also be in us so that the world may believe that
you have sent me.'

John 17:21 [NIV]

Since the Trinity was a hard concept for many to grasp,
St Patrick explained how God could be both three and one
using a shamrock leaf. The Celts' love of the Trinity can
be seen in many of their prayers:

I lie down this night with God,
And God will lie down with me;
I lie down this night with Christ
And Christ will lie down with me;
I lie down this night with the Spirit,
And the Spirit will lie down with me;
God and Christ and the Spirit
Be lying down with me.

Carmina Gadelica

I bless the Three in One
And the One in Three
Father
Spirit
Son
Thank you
for loving
me.

Liz Babbs

Father Spirit Son, you care for me.
Father Spirit Son, you protect me.
Father Spirit Son, you guide me.
Father Spirit Son, you love me.

Liz Babbs

Many Celtic religious communities today, as in the past, have a 'Rule' or way of living even if they live as dispersed communities. Roy Searle of The Northumbria Community writes:

A Rule of Life provides a framework, a rhythm and balance of prayer and action, work and rest, study and reflection, productivity and play, cell and community. Where we are both alone and together, where the relationship between solitude and hospitality is exercised, where serving has priority over consuming, where authenticity reigns rather than image. A Rule of Life reminds us of the importance of relationships mattering more than reputation, where we cultivate generosity as opposed to calculating control, where we care for creation, express a commitment to the poor, welcome the marginalized and become a voice for the voiceless.

The Aidan and Hilda Community, which draws inspiration from saints of those names, has adapted the traditional monastic vows of poverty, chastity and obedience. Its members live a ten-fold Way of Life based on these principles.

Exploring a new monasticism is the Northumbria Community who have a Rule of Life based on the values of Availability and Vulnerability. They have been influenced and informed on their journey by various sources, including the writings of Dietrich Bonhoeffer:

**The renewal of the Church will come from a new kind of monasticism which only has in common with the old an uncompromising allegiance to the Sermon on the Mount.**

DIETRICH BONHOEFFER

# GENEROUS hospitality

**W**hen we think of hospitality now we think of entertaining family and friends, but the biblical model of hospitality crosses all social boundaries. Jesus shocked his critics by eating 'with tax collectors and sinners' (Matthew 9:11). The monastic tradition continues to seek to practise God's welcome to the stranger, receiving guests as though they were Christ. The Rule of St Benedict 53:1– 2 states:

> All guests who present themselves are to be welcomed as Christ, for he himself will say: *I was a stranger and you welcomed me* (Matthew 25:35). Proper honour must be shown *to all, especially to those who share our faith* (Galatians 6:10) and to pilgrims.

**Don't forget to show hospitality to strangers, for some who have done this have entertained angels without realizing it!**
**HEBREWS 13:2 [NLT]**

69

The welcoming of Christ in the stranger is echoed in this ancient Celtic rune of hospitality:

> We saw a stranger yesterday
> We put food in the eating place,
> Drink in the drinking place,
> Music in the listening place,
> And with the sacred name of the triune God
> He blessed us and our house,
> our cattle and our dear ones.
> As the lark says in our song:
> Often, often, often goes the Christ
> In the stranger's guise.

With all the dangers of the road, in offering hospitality monastic communities would have saved peoples' lives. In so doing, they were embodying the message of The Good Samaritan, a story Jesus told about an outsider who took care of a traveller beaten up by robbers on the road. The following message that welcomes strangers to a crofter's door in Wales extends the same hospitality today:

> Hail Guest, we know not whom thou art.
> If friend, we greet thee with hand and heart,
> If stranger, such no longer be,
> If foe, our love will conquer thee.

May the road rise up to meet you;
may the wind be always at your back.
May the sun shine warm on your face
and the rain fall softly on your fields.
Until we meet again,
May God hold you
in the hollow of his hand.

AN IRISH BLESSING

Listening with sensitivity was an important part of hospitality, because in listening to another person they were also listening to God. The monks were trained to hear God and to have a deep attentiveness to all of life. In sharing God's love they not only opened their homes to a stranger, but their hearts too. Many travellers would have been spiritual seekers and it was in living alongside the monks in community, that they became followers of Christianity.

Love of God
Help me to be kind
To see the needs of the poor.
Spirit of God
Help me
To be
l
e
s
s
So that I might see
You more.

LIZ BABBS

# CELEBRATING LIFE

C. S. Lewis described joy as 'the serious business of heaven'. But joy and celebration is also integral to our earthly life and is characteristic of abundant living. Joy is not the same as happiness, which can be fleeting and temporary; joy is a gift that comes from knowing God and can overflow into every area of our lives. The Celts not only believed this, but lived it out in feasting and celebrating:

> **Sing to God a brand new song. He's made a world of wonders.**
> **PSALM 98:1 [TM]**

It was the time for a night feasting... a time when the people forgot the hard conditions of their lives and joy in one another's company; in rustic mirth, in music and dancing and the telling of tales told or song of the bards. The farm workers and folk from the village gathered in the great barn of the monastery. The space round the fire was left empty for the visiting bard.

ANNE WARIN

St Brigid of Ireland used to sing and pray in the kitchen as she baked for guests. Her joy in entertaining is expressed in this prayer attributed to her:

**I would prepare a feast and be host to the great High King, with all the company of heaven. The sustenance of pure love be in my house, the roots of repentance in my house. Baskets of love be mine to give, with cups of mercy for all the company. Sweet Jesus, be there with us, with all the company of heaven. May cheerfulness abound in the feast, the feast of the great High King, my host for all eternity.**

Joy is also part of the abundant life God promises in John's Gospel: 'I come that you might have life, and have it to the full' (John 10:10). Since the Celts were particularly drawn to the teachings of John they believed God wanted them to celebrate, because having fun is a hallmark of a vibrant community.

> **Joy of the Creator Father**
> **Joy of the Redeemer Son**
> **Joy of the Sustaining Spirit**
> **Joy of the Three in One.**
>
> LIZ BABBS

There is joy too in adopting a simple lifestyle, uncluttered by materialism. By living simply, the Celts were able to appreciate more fully the generosity and abundance of God. They thanked God for everything in their daily lives; the sunrise, the provision of food and the blessing of friends:

> Bless to us, O God
> The morning sun that is above us,
> The good earth that is beneath us,
> The friends that are around us,
> Your image deep within us,
> The day which is before us.
>
> ST PATRICK

**Thankfulness and prayer belong together... The simple enjoyment of our Lord is in itself a most blessed form of thanksgiving.**

ST JULIAN OF NORWICH

The rhythm of life and the joy of the seasons were also important to the Celts. They were naturally in tune with creation's rhythm, because they lived and worked on the land. Life was not seen as linear, but continuous and seasonal, like the ebb and flow of the tide. In a similar way, they did not see a separation between time and eternity, but saw eternity in every day. Like the Celtic knot, there was no beginning or end, death was part of life. This wonderful prayer, attributed to St Aidan, expresses the timeless continuity of God:

> God be with you in every pass,
> Jesus be with you on every hill,
> Spirit be with you on every stream,
> Headland and ridge and lawn;
> Each sea and land,
> Each moon and meadow,
> Each lying down, each rising up,
> In the trough of the waves,
> On the crest of the billows,
> Each step of the journey you go.
>
> Passionately and unconditionally
> God loves.
> Completely and utterly
> God loves.
> Now and forever
> God loves.

LIZ BABBS

We can learn so much from the Celtic way. It is an inclusive and holistic spirituality that recognizes the importance of equality and justice, honours creation and models the love of God and each other. The Celts have much to teach us about community and prayer, about hospitality and generosity, and about simplicity and celebration. While much of the West values money, fame, power and success, unearthing these precious treasures from the Celtic Christian tradition can enrich and transform our lives. For the Bible reminds us 'your heart will always be where your treasure is.' (Matthew 6:21).

**See that you be at peace among yourselves,**
**my children, and love one another,**
**follow the example of the good men of old,**
**and God will comfort you and help you,**
**both in this world**
**and the world to come.**

ATTRIBUTED TO ST COLUMBA

# bibliography

You can contact the author on liz@lizbabbs.com and find information on further resources via her website www.lizbabbs.com

Bede, *Ecclesiastical History of the English People*, (eds.) D. H, Farmer, R. E. Latham, (trans.) L. Shirley-Price, London: Penguin, 1955

Alexander Carmichael, *Carmina Gadelica – Hymns and Incantations,* Edinburgh: Floris Books, 1992

James Carney, *Medieval Irish Lyrics,* Dublin: Dolmen, 1967

Anthony P. Castle, *Quotes and Anecdotes – An Anthology for Preachers and Teachers*, Essex: Kevin Mayhew, 1979

*Celtic Prayers of Yesterday and Today,* Oxford: Lion Publishing, 1996

John O'Donohue, *Anam Cara – Spiritual Wisdom from the Celtic World*, London: Bantram Books, 1997

Timothy Fry (ed.), *The Rule of Saint Benedict in English*, Collegeville, MN: The Liturgical Press, 1982

Martin Guppy, *Guests – In Celebration of Celtic Hospitality*, Norwich: SCM Canterbury Press, 2000

Fiona MacLeod, *The Divine Adventure: Iona*, New York: Duffield, 1910

John T McNeill, *The Celtic Churches: A History A.D. 200 to 1200*, Chicago and London: The University of Chicago Press, 1974

The Northumbria Community, *Celtic Daily Prayer*, London: HarperCollins, 2000

Ray Simpson, *Celtic Daily Light*, Suffolk: Kevin Mayhew Ltd, 2003

Ray Simpson, *Exploring Celtic Spirituality* [new edition with study guide], Suffolk: Kevin Mayhew Ltd, 2004

*Holy Island Prayer Book*, Norwich: SCM Canterbury Press, 2002

Robert Van de Weyer, *Celtic Fire – An Anthology of Celtic Literature*, London: Darton, Longman and Todd, 1990

Hannah Ward, Jennifer Wild (compilers), *The Lion Christian Quotation Collection,* Oxford: Lion, 1997

Anne Warin, *Hilda: An Anglo-Saxon Chronicle*, London: Marshall Pickering, 1989